Suzukawa

Suzukawa

...his search for truth in photography

 The World Publishing Company / Cleveland and New York

Published by The World Publishing Company
2231 West 110th Street, Cleveland, Ohio 44102

Published simultaneously in Canada by
Nelson, Foster & Scott Ltd.

Library of Congress Catalog Card Number: 66–28442

Printed in the United States of America

Comments on Suzukawa

The attachment of pictures to words, and to specific ideas embodied in words, has always been uncertain and uneasy. The painful efforts of the historian-critic to pin down the *meaning* of a visual image, the philosophizing of the aesthetician *around* pictures, and the simple use of pictures to illustrate a verbal concept —all face an ultimately unsolvable problem. The meaning of the picture is in the picture, in its simple or complex visual image. This does not mean that the attempts are totally useless and should cease. Quite the contrary, by conscious effort words can help, can cut away at the fringes of hidden visual meaning, can circumscribe the essential core of the work of art. But the core remains, a profoundly varied and moving visual message, unknowable to language and untranslatable into words. Heine's lines still apply: "I am a picture. Do not ask me to speak."

Here the artist-photographer Suzukawa attempts to bridge the gaps between words, ideas, and images. I think he is an artist, for I prefer the visual images. They speak directly, skillfully, and with remarkably varied means: lines, tones, colors, textures, all combined into satisfying total configurations. The remarkable variety of techniques and effects available to the artist-photographer are used here with telling visual impact. The picture sequence alone is a lesson in photography as an art and is yet another testimonial that the little black box produces much, much more than mere records. Such effects are the result of initial selection, but, even more, of artful manipulation of the negative and print.

The artist's words must remain as personal notes, hints as to what his work means to him—but after the visual image was born. Sometimes, as in "tangerine," the connection is literal and elementary; at other times, as in "reaching through space," or "journey continuing endlessly," the photographer's general flavor seems to parallel the meaning of the words; at still others, the connection seems too ambiguous. My own feeling is that the old classical, then humanist, concept of *ut pictura poesis,* "as is painting so is poetry," both arts being addressed to the mind and the imagination, with its varied applications in the works of Poussin and Guercino, for example, is closer to a meaningful relationship of word, thought, and picture than that achieved by a more intuitive Oriental mode most typically expressed in Zen thoughts and images. After all, since this latter approach is by definition ineffable and unknowable, it is perhaps best not to discuss it. Zen words and thoughts are presented here with Western photographic images. Both sets are specific, concrete, and at the same time loaded with overtones. The marriage is a difficult one and perhaps ill-fated.

SHERMAN E. LEE

Unique among contemporary camera artists, George Suzukawa creates a bridge linking diverse ancient artistic traditions with highly advanced technological methods. The ancient traditions are the heritage of his native Japan. The modern methods were perfected in his adopted America.

At the core of Suzukawa's distinctive expression is nature, transmuted and transcended, sifted through his highly refined artistic sensibility. His photographs, like the best nature drawings of the Orient, are conceptual images inspired though they may be by astute and subtle perceptions of nature's nuances.

The most memorable prints of his already distinguished career are assembled in this volume, which is in every sense an autobiographical essay.

Here we become aware of how this young artist draws power from emptiness, how he evokes an inner energy and an inner light through poetic intensity and technical mastery.

His Eastern heritage does not allow for the Western dichotomy separating man from other forms of nature. His grasp of Western tradition, however, prompts him, in contrast to classical Japanese artists, to use the human figure as the central theme of much of his work. But with him, unlike with classical Western artists, the figure is not a temple of beauty marching but a palace of beauty floating.

In his most poignant creations Suzukawa repeatedly asserts the oneness of physical and spiritual love, as did his ancestors, and in so doing he offers us an aspect of passion that is timeless and soundless instead of being full of sound and fury as it is apt to be today.

At times, his obsessive perfectionalism results in photographs of astonishing spontaneity (as in his visions of dancers). In other instances, he creates a super reality (as in his astonishing Strawberries print) that heightens our senses and borders on the fantastic.

Suzukawa's astonishing accomplishments project his pride in photography as an independent artistic medium that, in skilled hands such as his, is just beginning to reach creative equality with the older arts of drawing and painting.

In extending the potentialities of this very modern art, Suzukawa is not satisfied to rely on technical virtuosity, though he certainly displays that, but he continually turns to tradition—both Oriental and Occidental—in the sense of utilizing not what is dead but what is already living.

In these photographs invisible emotions share the stage with visible aspects of life. The camera has been liberated from being merely a recording instrument. Here it provides us with X rays of a soul.

HENRY J. SELDIS

In my search for truth, I wander through a world filled with unknown and mysterious beauty.

I begin to pursue the sensitive image and to approach the sublime . . . hours, days, and years pass, but in the world where I live with my subject, whether nature, birds, or a nude, only our mutual passion continues timelessly and soundlessly.

The pure moment arrives. I am inspired to see, to create without conscious activity of the will . . . and if, in the result, I find my soul embodied in my work, I am satisfied.

SUZUKAWA

Suzukawa

my search for truth begins

tranquility flowers upon the earth

quietly and reverently
I approach nature's mystery

time passes

loneliness enters my being

power is gained from the emptiness

the energy sets my desire aflame

unconscious,
I wander in the world of the absolute

painfully,
I search the depths of my mind

and free myself completely

I begin to awaken

the moment arrives

I see eternal beauty

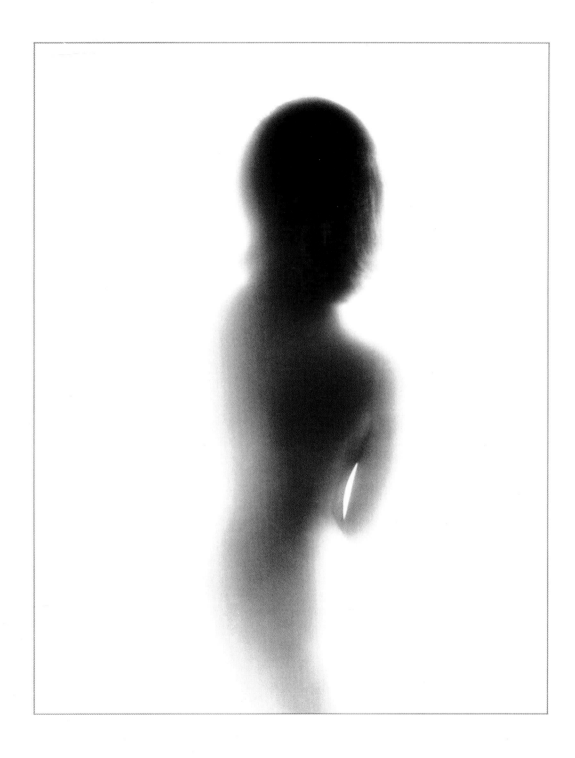

alive forever
in the abstraction of a form

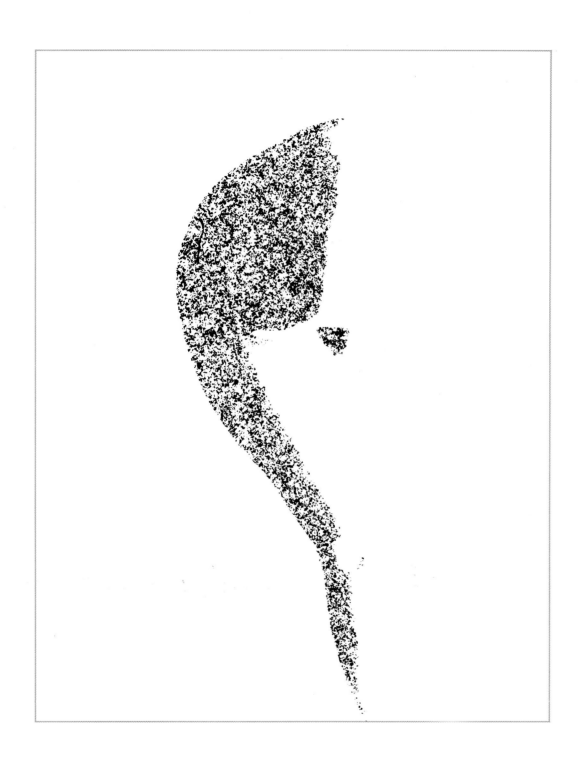

now I am one with my work

brightening the shadows of darkness

reaching through infinite space

my journey continues endlessly

searching for the essence of beauty

within the unknown world

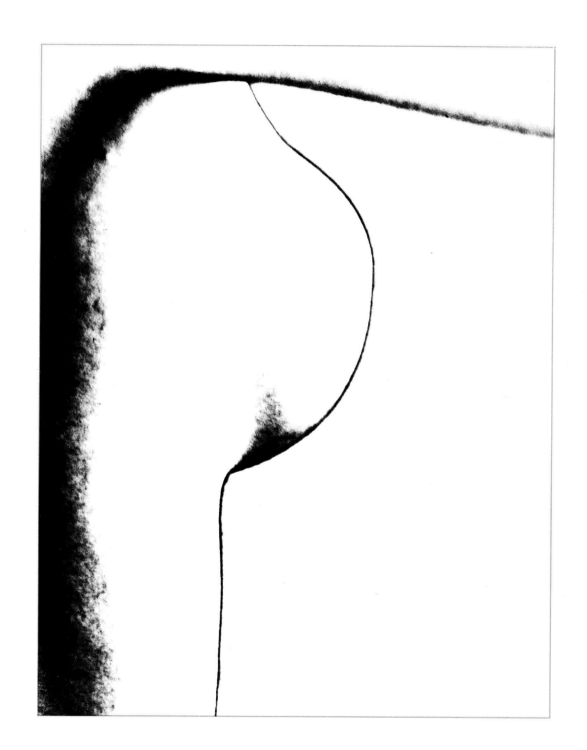

I perceive sublime truth

I am inspired by floating images

I discover the blue

colors...

tangerine, tangerine, tangerine...

and my soul.

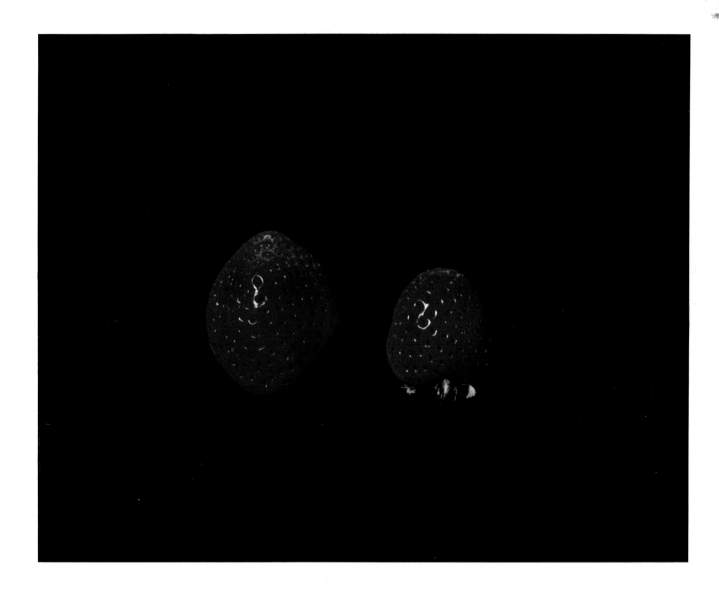

This book was set in Mistral and Optima by Boro Typographers. It was printed in six colors by Copifyer Lithographic Corporation and was bound by The World Publishing Company.